OUTDOOR SCIENCE

WEATHER

Sonya Newland

WAYLAND
www.waylandbooks.co.uk

First published in Great Britain in 2019 by Wayland

Produced for Wayland by
White-Thomson Publishing Ltd
www.wtpub.co.uk

Editor: Sonya Newland
Design: Rocket Design (East Anglia) Ltd
Illustrations: TechType
Consultant: James Thomson

ISBN: 978 1 5263 0944 0 (hbk)
ISBN: 978 1 5263 0945 7 (pbk)
10 9 8 7 6 5 4 3 2 1

Wayland
An imprint of
Hachette Children's Group
Part of Hodder & Stoughton
Carmelite House
50 Victoria Embankment
London EC4Y 0DZ

An Hachette UK Company
www.hachette.co.uk
www.hachettechildrens.co.uk

Printed in China

Picture acknowledgements:
Alamy: Novarc Images 23tr; Big Blu Books: Mia France 12–13 (all), Sonya Newland 24t, 28t; iStock: fotojog 20t; Shutterstock: Mike Mareen cover tl, 10t, Bas Meelker cover tr, Allen Paul Photography cover bl, DR-Images cover br, liseykina 4tl, Diane Diedrich 4tm, Krivosheev Vitaly 4tr, Ingrid Maasik 4bl, struvictory 4bm, stoaphoto 4br, mandritoiu 5t, humbak 5b, Igor Podgorny 6t, Michael Urmann 6b, Bernat Garcia Chamorro 7tl, Maksimilian 7tr, fokke baarssen 7b, Hachi888 8t, Soleil Nordic 10b, Zilvers 11tl, idiz 11tr, Zurijeta 11b, Chulkova Nina 14, Gabiele Maltinti 15tl, G.K. 15tr, CE Photography 15ml, Korionov 15mr, paul Prescott 15bl, IS MODE 15br, Carsten Medom Madsen 16t, Alexandra Theile 18tl, olenaa 18tr, Alexey Kljatov 18b, Stu Shaw 19t, Ken Tannenbaum 19b, Andrew Chin 22tl, Andreas Politis 22tml, Sasa Prudkov 22tmr, Sabphoto 22tr, bubblea 22b, Dark Moon Pictures 23tl, A. Bisogni 23b, Iavizzara 26t, Leonard Zhukovsky 26b, Designua 27t, StevenKingArt 27b.

Illustrations on pages 8, 9, 16, 17, 20, 21, 24, 25, 28 and 29 by TechType.

All design elements from Shutterstock.

Contents

What is weather?

Weather is the name for the conditions outside.

Different every day

What is the weather like today? What was it like yesterday?
In some places, the weather is always changing. It can change
by the day – or even by the minute!

Is the weather …

sunny?

windy?

stormy?

cloudy?

rainy?

snowy?

Seasons

There are four seasons. The weather usually changes between seasons.

In winter, it is often cloudy, windy or rainy. Temperatures are low. If it gets really cold, it may snow.

In spring, the weather is often mixed. It may be sunny or rainy. Temperatures are usually mild.

In summer, it is often sunny. Temperatures are warm or hot.

Autumn is like spring, with mixed weather and cooler temperatures.

What causes weather?

All around our planet is a layer of gases. This is called Earth's atmosphere. The Sun warms the air in the atmosphere to different temperatures in different places. The air begins to move. We call this wind. Wind causes different weather.

HANDS on!

Make a weather station out of pine cones. Collect four or five pine cones and line them up on an outside window ledge. In dry weather, the cones will open up. When rain is on the way, they will close.

Windy weather

Wind is the movement of air around the Earth.

What is wind?

Wind is caused when air in the atmosphere is heated by the Sun. The warm air rises. As it rises, cooler air replaces it. We feel this movement of air as wind.

What signs can you see of the wind in action?

Sea breezes

A sea breeze is a light wind that develops along the coast. The air above the land near the sea is warmed by the Sun. As it heats up, it rises. To replace the air lower down, air is pulled in from over the sea. As air moves inland, it creates a cooling breeze.

rising warm air

cooling breeze

The Beaufort scale

People who study the weather are called meteorologists. These experts measure wind using the Beaufort scale. This gives the wind a number from 0 to 12 depending on how fast it is travelling. The Beaufort scale also describes conditions on land and at sea. For example, at Number 7, it says:

On land: Whole trees in motion.

At sea: Sea heaps up and white foam from breaking waves begins to be blown in streaks.

Wind power

Wind is very important to humans because it is a renewable resource. That means we can use it to create energy because it will never run out. We use wind to turn huge turbines. These turbines produce electricity.

SPOT IT!

What effect is the wind having on the trees outside?

Wind energy is 'clean' energy – it does not pollute the air.

Make an anemometer

Scientists measure wind speed using an anemometer. Here's how to make your own anemometer.

You will need:
- ✴ five paper cups
- ✴ a hole punch
- ✴ three thin wooden dowels
- ✴ sticky tape
- ✴ sand
- ✴ an empty plastic 2-litre bottle

Step 1

Punch a hole near the top of four of the paper cups. On the fifth cup, punch four evenly spaced holes near the top. This is your centre cup.

centre cup

Step 2

Slide two of the wooden dowels through the centre cup so they form a cross, with the cup in the middle. Then fix the four other cups at each end of the wooden dowels using tape.

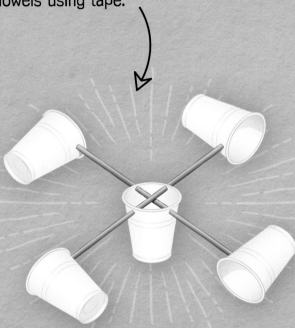

Step 3

Push the third dowel up through the bottom of the centre cup until it meets the middle of the cross and tape it in place. Pour some sand into the bottle to create a steady base, then push your anemometer into the sand.

Step 4

Put your anemometer outside and notice how fast or slow it spins depending on the wind speed. Take it to different places. How fast does it spin in each location? Try it at the top of a hill and at the bottom. What's the difference? Why do you think that is?

WHY NOT TRY?

Create wind using a piece of card. Wave it near your anemometer. How fast does it go? Now try it with a hairdryer or a fan. Does it go faster?

Sunshine and shadows

The Sun is always in the sky - even when you can't see it.

Making rainbows

Sunlight looks white, but it is made up of lots of different colours. When light passes through raindrops, the light is refracted (bent) and splits into different colours. We see this as a rainbow.

The curved Earth

The Sun doesn't heat Earth the same amount all over. Because the Earth has a curved surface, the Sun's rays hit some parts of the planet before others. The widest part of the Earth is the equator. The Sun's rays reach here first.

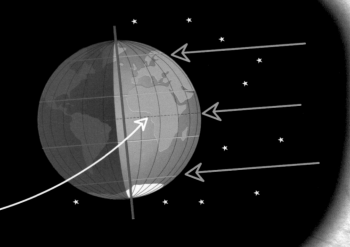

Places on or near the equator are usually warmer than elsewhere.

Heat waves and droughts

A heat wave is when an area gets a longer than normal period of hot weather. A drought is a long period of time when no rain falls. Both these types of weather can be dangerous.

Heat waves may cause wildfires, which can blaze out of control.

During a drought, the ground dries up and cracks. Nothing can grow.

Casting shadows

Shadows form when sunlight hits a solid object. The light cannot travel though the object, so a dark area appears on the ground on the opposite side of the object.

SPOT IT!

Next time you go out, check your shadow. What shape is it?

When the Sun is low in the sky, shadows are long and thin.

Measuring shadows

Become a human sundial and see how shadows fall at different times of day.

You will need:
* a sunny, cloudless day
* chalk
* a friend
* a tape measure
* a notebook and pencil

Step 1

Find a large open area that you can draw on with chalk, such as the playground or a patio. Mark an X in the middle of the area with the chalk. This is where you'll stand.

Step 2

Throughout the day, go outside every two hours and stand on the X. Get your friend to draw around your shadow with the chalk. Trace your shadow at least five times throughout the day.

Step 3

Each time you go outside, measure your shadow and write down how long it is. Also make a note of roughly where in the sky the Sun is. Try to guess what size your shadow will be when you next measure it.

Step 4

At the end of the day, look at your results. You should notice:

✳ When the Sun is low in the sky – in the morning and evening – it creates long, thin shadows.

✳ The higher in the sky the Sun is, the smaller the shadow.

✳ At midday, when the Sun is directly overhead, there is no shadow.

⊘ REMEMBER

✳ Never look directly at the Sun – it can damage your eyesight.

Clouds and rain

Rain is vital to our planet. Without it, there would be no life on Earth.

The water cycle

The way that water moves around the Earth is called the water cycle.

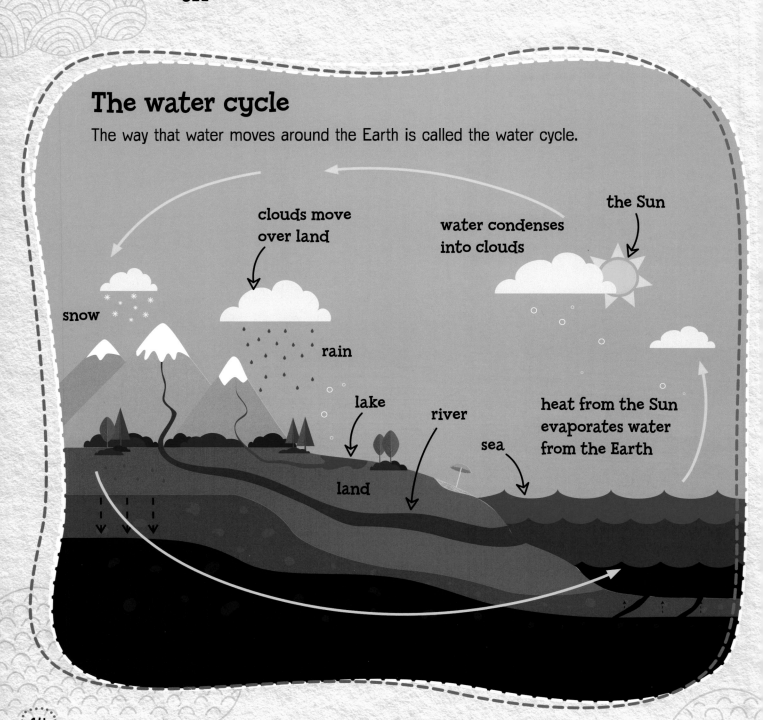

clouds move over land

water condenses into clouds

the Sun

snow

rain

lake

river

sea

heat from the Sun evaporates water from the Earth

land

What makes clouds?

Clouds are made of drops of water. Warm air containing water vapour rises, then cools high in the air. The water vapour condenses into water droplets.

Clouds look white on a sunny day because light from the Sun is white.

Clouds look grey when it rains because the water droplets in the cloud are bigger. They block out more of the light from the Sun.

There are different types of cloud. Can you see why they got their names?

cirrus
(meaning 'tuft')

cumulus
(meaning 'heap')

stratus
(meaning 'layer')

nimbus
(meaning 'rain-bearing')

SPOT IT!

What type of clouds can you spot in the sky today?

Evaporation in action

See how evaporation works with this puddle experiment.

You will need:
* a tape measure
* a piece of chalk
* a notebook and pencil

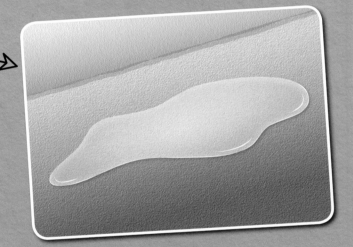

Step 1

Go outside when the Sun has come out after a rain shower. Find a medium-sized puddle on the pavement or other hard surface.

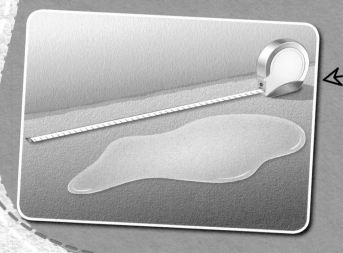

Step 2

Using the tape measure, measure how wide the puddle is and how long it is. Make a note of the measurements in your notebook.

Step 3

Draw round the outside of the puddle with your chalk. Look at how big it is now. What do you think you will see if you return to your puddle in an hour? Write down your guess.

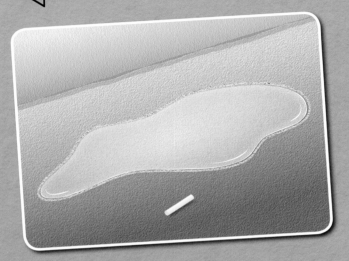

⚠ REMEMBER

✳ You'll need to wait until the rain has completely stopped before you start your experiment. Otherwise your puddle will get bigger not smaller!

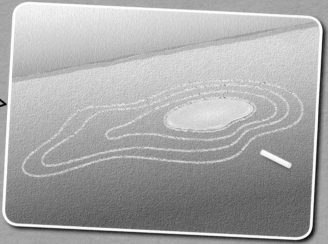

Step 4

Return to your puddle every hour. Draw round the puddle with chalk each time and measure how long and wide it is. What happens each time? Did you guess correctly?

Do the same experiment in different seasons or temperatures. Does the puddle evaporate more quickly when it is warmer or cooler?

Step 5

Look at the results of your experiment:

✳ How many hours does it take for your puddle to completely evaporate?

✳ Does the rate of evaporation speed up, slow down or stay the same throughout the process?

Snow and ice

When temperatures get very low, water freezes into snow and ice.

What is snow?

Sometimes the temperature in a cloud drops below freezing. When this happens, the droplets that make up the cloud turn to ice crystals. These ice crystals form snowflakes.

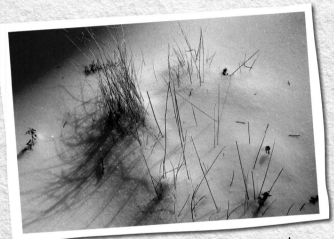

Sometimes snow is soft and powdery.

Sometimes it is wet and clumpy.

Amazing snowflakes

All snowflakes are a six-pointed shape. A single snowflake can contain as many as 200 crystals, arranged in a beautiful pattern.

Almost every snowflake has a different pattern.

SPOT IT!

Watch snowflakes gather on a window pane. Can you spot the six points of each flake?

In a blizzard, the snow is so thick and swirling that it may be impossible to see through it.

Blizzards

A blizzard is a bad snowstorm that lasts more than three hours. In a blizzard there are very high winds, which blow falling snow in all directions. The wind also picks up snow from the ground and sends it into the air.

Ice warning!

Sometimes the temperature drops quickly after it has rained. When this happens, ice forms on the ground. Rivers and lakes can freeze over. Ice may also fall from the sky in the form of freezing rain. This can develop into an ice storm.

'Black ice' is a thin layer of clear ice that forms on roads in very cold weather. It is especially dangerous because it is hard to see.

Melting ice

When it is snowy or icy, people put salt on the roads. Find out why with this experiment.

You will need:
* a shallow plastic container
* water
* a freezer
* salt
* a notebook and pencil

Step 1

Pour the water into the plastic container. Use just enough to create a thin layer of water, about 0.5 cm, at the bottom of the tub. Put the container in the freezer overnight.

Step 2

In the morning, take the container outside. Tap the bottom and pull the edges to loosen the frozen water. Carefully remove the sheet of ice and place it on a surface outside, like a wall or a table.

Step 3

Sprinkle some salt on to your ice sheet. What happens? Make a note in your notebook. Watch the ice for at least ten minutes to see how the salt affects it. Listen to the noises it makes as well as looking at how the ice changes.

Step 4

Repeat the experiment, but this time stir some salt into the water in the tub before you freeze it. What difference does this make? Does it take longer to freeze? Does it take less time to melt?

What's happening?

Water freezes at 0°C. This is called its freezing point. Salt lowers the freezing point of water. So, when snow falls on salt, it starts to melt. Putting salt on the roads also stops ice forming because the water will not freeze unless it is much colder.

WHY NOT TRY?

Put a banana in the freezer and leave it overnight. In the morning you'll find the banana is as hard as a hammer! That's because the water in the banana has frozen solid.

Thunder and lightning

A thunderstorm is no ordinary storm. It is an electric storm.

What do you see and hear during a thunderstorm?

wind?

thunder?

rain?

lightning?

Lightning flashes

Lightning is a bright flash of electricity in the sky. During a storm, water drops in clouds turn to ice. They move very quickly, bumping into each other. As they bump, they create an electric charge. Eventually, the electricity builds up so much it creates a flash of lightning.

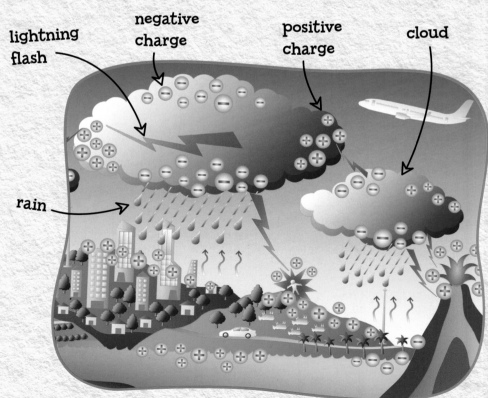

lightning flash

negative charge

positive charge

cloud

rain

Types of lightning

Forked lightning is when the flash of electricity zig-zags to the ground.

Sheet lightning is when the flash is near the horizon. It seems to light up the whole sky.

Thunder rolls

The electricity also creates a clap of thunder. You hear the thunder after you see the lightning because sound travels more slowly than light. Lightning can travel at nearly 10 million metres per second. Thunder only travels at about 340 metres per second.

Thunder seems to 'roll' for a few seconds. That's because it echoes off the ground, hills or buildings.

HANDS On!

Work out how far away a storm is by counting the seconds between the lightning flash and the thunder roll. It is one mile (1.6 km) for every five seconds you count.

! REMEMBER

If you are caught outside in a storm:

✳ Stay away from trees and telegraph poles – they are tall so they may get hit by lightning.

✳ Stay away from water – water conducts electricity.

Make a rain gauge

Work out the rainfall in your area by making a rain gauge.

You will need:
* an empty plastic bottle
* scissors
* masking tape
* a ruler
* a waterproof marker pen
* a notebook and pencil

Step 1

Cut the top off the bottle. Place it upside down inside the body of the bottle to create a sort of funnel. Tape it in place.

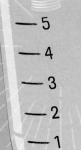

Step 2

Using the ruler, create a gauge up the side of the bottle, marking off in centimetres from the bottom with the marker pen.

Step 3

Put the bottle in an open space outside. You can bury it in soil to keep it steady.

Step 4

At the same time each day, go out and see how much rain has collected in your rain gauge. Note down the date and the amount of rainfall every day. You could design a table to record your results, or you could draw a graph to see how the rainfall changes over a period of time.

WHY NOT TRY?

Measure the rain in the gauge after a series of rain showers. Time how long each rain shower lasts. Compare the amount of rain to the length of the shower. Was it short and heavy or long and light?

⚠ REMEMBER

* You need to empty the rain gauge when you have taken your measurement so you get a fresh reading the next day.

Wild weather

Some parts of the world have even more extreme weather ...

Huge hurricanes

A hurricane is a huge tropical storm. The biggest hurricanes can be up to 650 km wide. They form out at sea, but can move on to land. The very centre of a hurricane is called the 'eye'. In the eye, it is perfectly calm. Hurricanes are also known as cyclones and typhoons.

Winds in a hurricane blow in a circle. North of the equator they blow anticlockwise. South of the equator they blow clockwise.

Hurricanes can cause severe damage and flooding.

Naming hurricanes

Meteorologists know when a hurricane is coming and they give each one a name. The name of the first hurricane in a year begins with A. The next begins with B, and so on. They alternate between boy and girl names. If a storm causes a lot of damage and loss of life, that name is not used again.

Tornadoes

A tornado is another very strong windstorm. Tornadoes are much smaller than hurricanes, and they usually form on land. A tornado occurs when cold winds high up meet warmer winds lower down. When this happens, air is pushed together and swirls upwards very quickly. It forms a kind of funnel that moves along the ground. As tornadoes move around, they can suck up objects in their path.

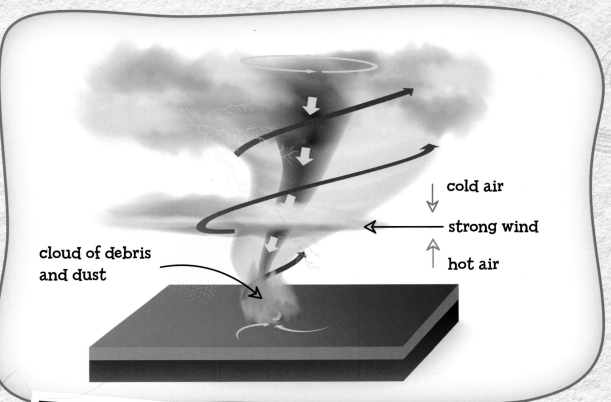

cloud of debris and dust

cold air

strong wind

hot air

Tornadoes, or twisters, are much smaller than hurricanes – usually only up to 45 m wide.

SPOT IT!

Can you spot mini tornadoes on a windy day? Look at how leaves blow in circles.

Make a wind catcher

Even light winds can gather up objects as they blow. Make a wind catcher to see what the wind carries.

You will need:

※ four plastic lids

※ scissors

※ pieces of string

※ petroleum jelly

※ a notebook and pencil

Step 1

Using the scissors, make a small hole near the edge of one of the lids. Thread the string through the hole to create a loop, then tie a knot to secure it. Do the same with the other three lids.

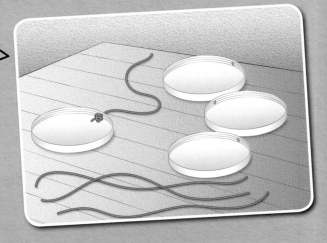

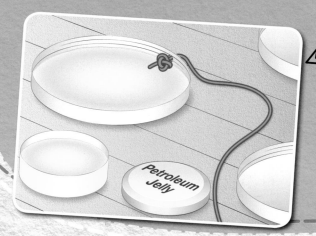

Step 2

Cover one side of each lid with petroleum jelly. This will act as a kind of glue to catch things blown around by the wind.

Step 3

Hang your lids outside on a windy day. Put each one in a different place. Leave them for about two hours, then bring them inside to see what they've collected. Note down what you find for each catcher. You might find:

* seeds * leaves * dirt * bugs
* hair or fur * small twigs

Step 4

Repeat the experiment on days when the wind is different strengths. Try a day when there are only light breezes, a gusty day when branches are moving around, and a really windy day when the trees themselves seem to be swaying. What do you notice about:

* the type of objects your wind catchers collect?
* the amount of material they collect?

WHY NOT TRY? Ask your friends to put up their own wind catchers. Compare your findings. If they are different, why do you think that is?

! REMEMBER

* Get an adult to help you make the holes in the lids.

Glossary

alternate – swapping from one to the other and back again

anemometer – a device that measures wind speed

atmosphere – the layer of gases that surrounds the Earth

Beaufort scale – a scale that indicates how strong wind is

condense – to change from a gas to a liquid and form droplets

electric charge – a tiny amount of electricity

equator – an imaginary line round the middle of the Earth, the same distance from the North and South Poles

evaporate – to turn from a liquid to a gas

freezing – changing from a liquid to a solid

gauge – a device that measures something

meteorologist – a scientist who studies the weather

pollute – to poison something such as air or water by putting harmful substances into it

refracted – when light bends as it passes from one material to another

renewable resource – a resource such as the Sun and wind that will never run out

turbine – a type of rotary engine that creates energy by turning a fan of blades

vapour – a substance in the form of a gas

wildfire – a fire that starts naturally and spreads quickly

further reading

Books

Weather and Seasons (Curious Nature)
by Nancy Dickmann (Franklin Watts, 2017)

Weather (Our Earth in Action)
by Chris Oxlade (Franklin Watts, 2014)

Weatherwise series
(Wayland, 2014)

Websites

This website, run by a meteorologist, has facts and fun projects to help you find out more about weather.
www.weatherwizkids.com/

This website has links to all sorts of weather information and experiments.
www.metoffice.gov.uk/learning/weather-for-kids

Find out all about weather with this interactive website.
www.dkfindout.com/uk/earth/weather/

Index

OUTDOOR SCIENCE

Titles in the series

MATERIALS

What are materials?
Wonderful wood
Build a lolly stick raft
Mighty metal
Rugged rock
Make a sedimentary rock
Super soil
Separate soil
Man-made materials
Test waterproof materials
Solids, liquids and gases
Changing state
Make an ice sculpture

PLANTS

What are plants?
Parts of a plant
Comparing plants
Super seeds
Going underground
Growing up
'Crying' leaves
Pollinating plants
Build a bee hotel
All about trees
How old is that tree?
Fruit and vegetables
Create your own garden

ANIMALS

Animals everywhere
Types of animals
Make a paint trap
Animals in the earth
Bug hunting
Awesome insects
Plant a butterfly habitat
Hard-to-spot animals
Nocturnal animal spotting
Amazing amphibians
Tracking tadpoles
In the air
Name that song

HABITATS

What are habitats?
What lives where?
Animal identification
Food chains
Habitat hunting
What's in the pond?
Make a mini-pond
Log life
Minibeast hunt
Rock pools
Name that shell!
In the grass
Be a habitat hero

WEATHER

What is weather?
Windy weather
Make an anemometer
Sunshine and shadows
Measuring shadows
Clouds and rain
Evaporation in action
Snow and ice
Melting ice
Thunder and lightning
Make a rain gauge
Wild weather
Make a wind catcher

FORCES

What are forces?
Measuring forces
Playground forces
Forces and motion
Make a bottle rocket
Attractive gravity
Spin the bucket
Surface friction
Testing surfaces
Air and water resistance
Make an egg parachute
Amazing magnetism
Make a compass